IS YOUR COACH BONA FIDE OR A BONEHEAD?

by

Tommy Coleman

Dorrance Publishing Co
585 Alpha Drive
Suite 103
Pittsburgh, PA 15238
Visit our website at *www.dorrancebookstore.com*

ISBN: 979-8-8852-7117-2
eISBN: 979-8-8852-7844-7

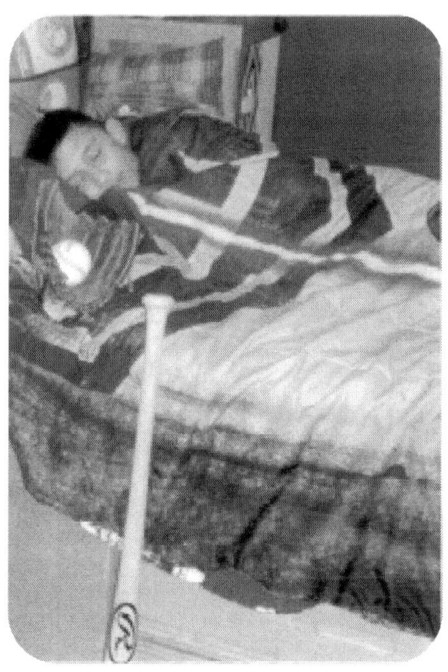

"When boys cease going to bed with a ball under their pillow and a bat near the bed, something beautiful will be lost forever from the American way of life."

– Ford Frick (Former Commissioner of Baseball).

CONTENTS

PROLOGUE

My purpose in writing this book was twofold.

First, to educate those who are just beginning to coach in the physical and emotional fundamentals involved. To point out some of the opportunities for self-improvement and to suggest methods for proper education of the young people you will be charged with. To use your powers of observation and experimentation to improve your games as well as theirs. To make the game more enjoyable for all - players, coaches, officials, and spectators and to assure that they go away with hearts full of great memories.

Second, to point out to parents some of the areas to be avoided when placing your children in the hands of someone who will be responsible for lessons that will be with their child for years to come. To be sure that the persons involved are acting in their child's best interest.

Most of my commentary relates to Baseball, but the basic philosophies of coaching will apply to other sports as well. With luck, some of those misguided individuals will see the error of their ways, overcome their arrogance and/or ignorance, and make the proper adjustments in their attitude.

I have coached with and against coaches of all types; some good, some bad. I was able to experience firsthand, some of the types I consider a "bonehead," and many I respected and was able to learn a great deal from. A bonehead coach can teach you how not to do things.

PART 1

THE GAME THAT IS BASEBALL

"Baseball cannot change the world but it can change YOUR life!"

–Jackie Robinson

Baseball and life have much in common. Both are a process, and both are NOT fair! Life is a game that should be played by the rules, just like baseball. Baseball is a sport with a lot of ups and downs. It is emotionally and mentally challenging. We may learn many of life's little lessons from baseball, and hopefully these lessons will lead to a healthy and productive life.

Baseball is also about learning to deal with failure. In baseball, even the best fail more than they succeed. A hitter who fails seven out of 10 attempts is considered successful and a candidate for the Hall of Fame. A player who is afraid of failure will not go the extra mile, so to speak, and it could possibly cost them the next rung on the ladder of success. Quoting Babe Ruth: *"Never let the fear of striking out get in your way."*

Teach the kids to love the game, and they will love to learn the game. Making the game more fun to play will generate a great deal of interest in baseball, with a side benefit of healthier, happier kids and families. This logic can and does apply to any sport. Get the kids interested, teach them to love the game, to experience the thrill and the excitement, and every day they are involved with the game, they won't be out causing trouble.

More kids being brought back to the ballparks and off the streets leads to more public interest and appreciation of our national pastime, and of our youth as a whole. With a little luck, it also translates to fewer drug problems and a drop in juvenile delinquency.

When I see a "coach" who will put on a clinic for 30 or 40 kids, and charge them X amount of dollars for two or three hours, I feel sick and insulted for the game of baseball. Two or three hours is not enough time to teach kids how to play. You can tell them how to play, maybe give a few examples, but unless they can work at it over several days, most of it won't stick.

I have always regarded baseball as the great equalizer due to the fact that it doesn't matter if you are outweighed and outsized, the pitcher still has to throw strikes, and the batter has to hit good pitches. A good defense can counter a good offense;

good reflexes and quick hands can counter the 90 MPH fastball or the sharp breaking curve ball. Clever mixing of pitches and good control can nullify a good hitter.

Baseball is a game of wonders. It seems that in every game, you see something you've never seen before, and that is a primary appeal of the game. We've all seen dozens of leaping or diving catches, but each one is every bit as addicting as the previous one. There is little to comparison to the thunder from the crowd witnessing a bases-loaded, base-clearing double to the gap, or a perfectly executed suicide squeeze bunt, or the suspense in the air during a tremendous relay from the outfield to cut off a runner at third base or at the plate!

Baseball's strength has always been that one generation passed it on to the next, passing on its traditions and its secrets. The day's game can be a great opening for conversation with your child while playing catch and discussing the game. A game of catch can be soothing and relaxing. A game of catch is an essential gesture of parenthood when families are working well.

Nietzsche said there is nothing so serious as a child at play. Everyone tosses to be understood, and the best part of the game is the silence. I throw. He catches. He throws. I catch. The ball wobbles so slightly in the bright stillness that one can almost count the stitch. One throwing to the other in silence allows both to reflect on past and future thoughts of the game.

There are a series of games within each game of baseball. When a batter faces a pitcher, it is a challenge between getting on base or being put out.

When a batter becomes a baserunner, there is a game between the runner and the pitcher. The runner tries to distract the pitcher to assist the next batter. The pitcher tries to remove the runner from the base.

With runners on base, a larger game is played between the offense and the defense where the defense tries to keep the offense from advancing runners and scoring.

Nothing is simple about baseball. I believe it was Joe Garagiola who tried to explain the game simply when he wrote "A Simple Explanation of Baseball," which pretty well sums up what the game is all about.

This is a game played by two teams; one out, the other in. The one that's in sends players out one at a time to see if they can get in before they get out. If they get out before they get in, they come in, but it doesn't count. If they get in before they get out, it does count. When the ones out get three outs from the ones in before they get in without being out, the team that's out comes in, and the team in goes out to get those in out before they get in without being out. When both teams have been in and out nine times, the game is over. The team with the most in without being out before corning in wins unless the ones in are equal. In which case, the last ones in go out to get the ones in out before they get in without being out. The game ends when each team has the same number of ins and outs, but one team has more in without being out before coming in.

There will always be some very serious and pointed discussions about baseball. Who was the best hitter of all time, Ty Cobb or Pete Rose? Who was the most impressive home run hitter, Babe Ruth or Hank Aaron? What was the best team in history? The worst? There is no way everyone will ever agree one way or the other, but these are the type of arguments that keep baseball interesting and in the hearts of the fans.

For sake of argument, think about the following comparisons:

Comparison of At Bats for Cobb and Rose

	Cobb	Rose	Difference
At Bats	11,434	14,053	2,619
Hits	4,189	4,256	67
Hits Per At Bats	1 per 2.72	1 per 3.30	

If same number of at bats were figured in, Cobb would have had 962 more hits for a total of 5,151!

Comparison of Babe Ruth and Hank Aaron

	Aaron	Ruth	Difference
At Bats	12,364	8,399	3,965
Walks	1,402	2,056	

Home Runs	755	714	41
HRs Per At Bats	1 per 16.3	1 per 11.76	

If Ruth had the same number of AB's, he could have possibly hit 337 more home runs for a total of 1,051!

These are just some of the issues that keep baseball alive. There is always a new player or situation to get people excited, so there is never a shortage of subjects for discussion and debate.

Not being on a team does not mean they have failed as athletes. It just means that they have to find other pleasurable ways to continue enjoying their sports. Parents need to remind these kids of the fun they had playing these games and encourage them to find time to play them with family members and friends. Helping your kids stay connected to the sports they love now can encourage them to remain physically active throughout their lives.

THE CODE OF THE GAME

Baseball is a great platform for learning positive life skills that play a big part in making one a better student, worker, or citizen. The primary goal of playing baseball is to allow young children to grow up happy, productive, and creative, not for them to become big leaguers. If that happens, great; but that is not the goal.

There is an unwritten code that players should strive to live by and decent coaches should encourage.

Players should enjoy just picking up the ball, bearing in mind that the game will end, BUT life goes on. They should live clean and play hard. Be a gentleman and role model on and off the field, and always do the "right thing"!

Players must respect officials and accept their decisions and never forget that when people judge a player's actions, they judge not only the player, but the team, the league, the community the player represents, and the game itself.

The player must undergo hard training realizing there is no gain without pain.

The player must strive for team harmony and unity, recognizing the team pecking order, following the rule of sameness: Treat everybody the same.

Put family first and before sports, games, and other extracurricular activities.

Players should play for the love of the game, win without boasting, lose graciously without excuse, but never quit. Be concerned with sportsmanship FIRST! The root word of the word sportsmanship is sports, but that doesn't mean that sportsmanlike behavior is important only on athletic fields. In life, people who are honest, consistently give their best effort, don't make excuses, respect others, and are able to accept everyday outcomes without complaining have a better chance to succeed. They are the type of people who any wise CEO would want to build a company or organization around.

Because of their attitude, work ethic, and professionalism, those who consistently exhibit sportsmanlike behavior in the "real world" earn the respect of their peers, have many friends and admirers, and enjoy the highest level of job satisfaction. People will go out of their way to help make a good sport successful. They are people who can go to bed every night satisfied, knowing that they have given their best no matter the outcomes of that particular day.

SPORTSMANSHIP 101

When people think of sportsmanship, they naturally think about sports. Well, sportsmanship is defined in this way: Someone who plays fair, sticks to the rules, and accepts defeat without any rancor or bitterness. On the field, a good sport plays hard and tries his or her absolute best to win within the scope of the rules. A good sport doesn't complain to the officials, doesn't "trash talk," and helps an opponent who falls down get back to his or her feet.

When all is said and done, this person has no regrets. The athlete put forth his or her best effort and played fairly, earning the admiration and respect of teammates, coaches, officials, and opposing players. Despite being a true competitor, this person is willing to openly congratulate opponents and accept even the most bitter of outcomes because he or she knows that there was nothing more that could have been done within rules of the game to change the end result.

In life, each day presents many ups and downs. There are far more small defeats than major successes. Good sports don't get bogged down in these small setbacks. They accept the outcomes, acknowledge that someone might have had a better idea, and push on toward bigger and better things. For people of that mindset, success is right around the corner. For poor sports, there are nothing but excuses and complaints, which suck up energy and waste valuable time.

A good sport believes that his or her approach is the right one and will not resort to underhanded or deceitful tactics for the sake of improving the results. This person goes back to the drawing board and puts in the time necessary to achieve a more desirable outcome, confident that his or her approach will ultimately lead to success. Poor sports are easily frustrated and often resort to tactics that may prove successful in the short term but ultimately come back to haunt them.

Baseball has been a major passion in my life since I was seven years old. My mother and I never missed the Brooklyn Dodgers whenever they were on the "Game of the Week." As soon as I was big enough to ride my bicycle and keep up with my older brothers, I would follow along to the school yard a few blocks away and give my all to play with them.

My brothers did not try to discourage me, but they didn't cut me any slack either. If I wanted to play, I'd better stay up with them and take what happened without a lot of complaining. I was in Seventh Heaven when I was on that field, and it didn't matter how tired I got; there was no way I was going to complain.

When I got older, I was introduced to organized team play. I knew someday I'd be playing on the big fields, just like my brothers and like many young ball players, I dreamed of someday being in "the show," Major League Baseball. I had friends and brothers to play catch with or to organize our own neighborhood games. When we didn't have enough kids to play a game, we played Workup or 500, or we just played catch, a great time to work on our curve ball.

On weekends, some of us would climb over the walls at our local ballpark the morning after the local semipro team had played. We would find treasures from the night before. Things like broken bats, broken helmets, and once in a while, a forgotten cap. Such wonders!

The local Pepsi Cola distributor would come and service the concession stand while we were playing. He knew we were not hurting anything, so he would wait until he finished, then come out and tell us we were not supposed to be there. He would escort us out then drive away, knowing full well that as soon as he was out of sight, we were back over the fence again.

I was fortunate to learn under the generous tutelage of several caring men who were knowledgeable in the game and more than willing to share their knowledge with anyone interested. None of these men ever asked for a dime, and a lot of young boys learned how to play ball the right way for free. God alone knows what these men gave up for us. The treats they doled out alone had to add up.

The men who mentored us had a basic rule of thumb. All we had to do was listen, work at it, and respect the game. The coaches enjoyed watching us learn and grow in experience almost as much as we did. Their basic rule was:

When the game is fun, everybody involved has a good time.

Our small town came to develop some very strong teams over the years, and during the sixties, we had some very dominant teams. Some of the Babe Ruth and American Legion teams went all the way to the World Series tournaments. Twice, our American Legion squads finished second in the nation!

When I was in high school, I was pitching well. I had a good live fastball and a curve ball to die for. An injury to my pitching arm ended my quest for the varsity and cost me two years of American Legion ball, the end of my childhood dreams of the big leagues.

I was crushed, but my love for the game remained. I had to be a part of it. I tried umpiring, but that just didn't do it for me. I started coaching at the age of 25 and have been active at one level or another for the last 45 years. I have never been paid for any of my time, nor would I accept it. I believe the men who trained me did it for free, so what right would I have to extract money from a young kid who wanted to learn? When a young man comes up to me in the mall and says, "Hi Coach, remember me?" I could not ask for more in the way of compensation.

PART II

YOUTH SPORTS

Mr. Webster tells us that a game is "any form of play or way of playing; any specific amusement or sport involving physical and/or mental competition under specific rules." He tells us further that "to play is to amuse oneself, as by taking part in a game or a sport; to engage in recreation." Active kids maintain positive self-images, higher self-esteem, have higher levels of self-health awareness, and higher levels of motivation and confidence.

Children play sports to have fun, to be with friends and develop their skills. Studies show that they drop out when these needs are not being met. Children burning out on play makes no sense and should not be allowed to happen. When we take the fun out of sports, there is a strong chance that the kids will take themselves out of the games. Well trained and caring coaches will enhance enjoyment of the team sports experience for young players as well as veterans. Happy players will increase retention rates. Increase retention rates among participants and reduce sports-related injuries, and you will have a successful program.

Kids need time to be kids, especially in the summer. This includes going to the pool with friends, hanging out in the park playing pick-up games, riding their bikes through the neighborhood, or simply spending time at home with family.

Twenty million kids register each year for youth recreational and competitive sports, with approximately one third of children aged nine through 13 participating in some form of organized physical activity. Children play sports to have fun, be with friends, and develop their skills. In any youth sports program, the emphasis should be on the proper instruction of the fundamentals over winning, keeping the "fun" in fundamentals and developing a passion for the game. One of the most positive effects of youth sports is the increase in exercise and physical activity. Organized play, like that found through playing ball in the park or learning the rules of the game in physical education class, provides kids with an opportunity to build skills necessary for teamwork and to identify potential leadership traits.

Sports give young people a chance to run and develop their muscles, which improves their physical condition and improves a child's coordination. As a result, children who play sports are more likely to be physically fit, have a healthy weight, and maintain a better body image. According to Familyresources.com, youth who are involved in extracurricular sports show improvements in health, academic performance, and adjustment in later life.

It's important to understand all the benefits of youth sports, so you can take the initiative to get and keep your child actively involved. Remember, the #1 reason kids play sports is to have fun, not to win. While it is true kids like to win, study after study consistently shows that having fun is far more important than anything else—including winning.

Youth sports continue to be very popular. Unfortunately, more and more children are spending more of their time indoors playing video games or browsing the Internet. Too much time in front of a computer can lead to developmental problems. Sitting at a computer can promote bad posture if the child sits incorrectly. Schools have recess breaks to give young minds a break from study. A child is also at risk of not getting enough exercise if they spend several hours per day on the computer with no physical activity breaks.

Youth sports development generally proceeds through three distinct stages:

1. **The early years, or what has been labeled the Romance Phase.**

   In the early years (Romance Phase), the child develops a love for the activity, has a great deal of fun, receives encouragement from significant others, is free to explore the activity, and achieves a good deal of success. Parents also instill the value of hard work and doing things well during this time.

2. **The middle years, labeled the Precision Phase.**
   In the Precision Phase, an experienced coach or teacher promotes long-term systematic skill learning in the talented individual. The focus is on technical mastery, technique, and excellence in skill development.
3. **The later years, or the Integration Phase.**
   Finally, in the later years, or the Integration Phase, an individual continues to work with a master teacher (coach) and practices many hours a day to turn training and technical skills into optimal performance. There is a realization that the practiced activity is significant in one's life.

These phases occurred over a 15- to 20-year time period, and each person moves through each phase in a developmental sequence, without skipping phases.

KidsHealth.org warns parents that children in sports use high levels of energy and have an increased chance of injury, so it is important that they receive proper nutrition. Youth sports include a broad range of activities from archery to wrestling, some with extreme physical contact such as football and rugby and other non-contact sports that require more finesse and endurance, like tennis or track. There should be one common factor in all youth sports: Proper training for coaches should not only emphasize teaching young people about sports skills and lifetime physical activity, but also about responsible leadership, nonviolent conflict resolution, sportsmanship, integrity, and cooperation.

Most youth programs are run by volunteer organizations and, in some cases, are coached by volunteers who are somewhat inexperienced. Most of these individuals mean well and put a lot of time and effort into the programs they are involved with, but sadly, there are those who "slip through the cracks" and are a detriment to the sports and to the kids they mentor.

The opportunity to play in tournaments beyond league play is important. It gives the player valuable playing experience against the best players in the state, region, and nation. This also gives additional exposure to college and professional scouts. With luck, it can lead to a once-in-a-lifetime opportunity to play in a world series.

Anyone can improve over time, even athletic ability, if the player is inspired and willing to put forth the effort. Some players need only guidance and support; some need direction and discipline, while some may need extra time and effort. The good coach will recognize this and address it, while the poor coach will write the kid off as a lost cause.

PHYSICAL BENEFITS

Starting a child early in sports should be the beginning of a lifelong interest. Sports are competitive in nature, but they teach values to kids that will be useful for the rest of their lives. Active kids maintain positive self-images, and with improved self-esteem, higher levels of self-health awareness, motivation, and confidence are attained. Competitive sports require discipline and focus from children, especially as they grow older. Children who can keep their body focused on the sport may also have an easier time focusing their mind on schoolwork.

One of the best positive effects of youth sports is the increase in exercise and physical activity. It's very important for children to stay active and get enough movement and exercise to stay healthy. Participating in youth sports provides good exercise for an age group that is increasingly becoming overweight. A sport gives a kid a chance to run and develop stronger muscles while burning off excess fat, which improves physical condition. Playing sports, a child's coordination will improve.

According to SportMatters.ca, kids who are involved in sports generally live an overall healthier, happier lifestyle. Children who play sports are more likely to be physically fit, have a healthy weight, and maintain a better body image. A healthy body contributes to a healthy mind, and regular exercise contributes to overall physical and mental health.

Youth who are involved in extracurricular sports show improvements in health, academic performance, and adjustment in later life. These young people also have significant psychological benefits from participation in sports. School athletes are more likely to stay in school. Both male and female athletes have higher grades, higher educational aspiration, and less discipline problems in school.

A kid can be playing other sports and still improve as a baseball player. Better athletes generally are better baseball players, so participating in other sports can lead to gains in athleticism that are only going to benefit the kids. Playing other sports gives kids a break, prevents an attitude of boredom, and gives kids a chance to strengthen other muscles in their body.

In addition to the physical benefits that can be derived from participation in other sports, imagine how much a kid who loves baseball will look forward to next season after taking some time off from serious competition. Even elite, professional athletes require a period of time in which they maintain a certain level of fitness without continually using the muscles that are necessary to play their main sport.

Playing other sports throughout the year and not just concentrating on baseball is another important tool for preventing burnout. Playing other sports gives kids a break from baseball and leads to a greater appreciation for the game itself. Daniel Wann, a professor of psychology at Murray State University, recommends that kids really need to be encouraged to play different sports. Enabling kids to play other sports throughout the year and not just concentrate on one sport is an important tool for preventing burnout and serious injuries. There are two factors to support this statement. First, it allows the muscle groups used to play baseball to take a break. And second, it allows for other sports skills to be developed.

In addition, playing other sports develops athleticism, which will prove extremely beneficial on the baseball field. The footwork in soccer can be transferred very easily to basketball or baseball, and the starts and stops in basketball can be transferred to infielders or running the bases.

In some cases, kids are being forced to choose one sport over another when programs overlap or compete with each other. While there are some kids who are going to love the game so much that they will play it happily just about every day, for the vast majority of kids, a year-round commitment can lead to burnout.

Many medical experts fear that year-round participation in one sport is putting a strain on the developing bodies of young players. A report by James White and Gerald Masterson, PhD, advises parents to avoid pressuring children to specialize in just one sport, as this may make children feel they must perform rather than have fun. Instead, allow children to play all the different sports they wish. Also, create an environment for your child that decreases the competitive aspect of sports in favor of its fun and enjoyable aspects.

Participation in other sports allows the muscle groups used to play each sport to take a break, and it allows for other sports skills to be developed, creating a more rounded athlete. Using the same muscles over and over again without varied activity can introduce problems with the child's growth platelets. This kind of damage can persist into long term health issues.

MENTAL BENEFITS

Youth sports is an excellent opportunity to teach children about personal drive and healthy competitiveness that will help them later in life. Youth who play sports are able to use strategy more easily, as sports teach important values about teamwork, ethics, fair-play, sportsmanship, and encouragement, which will be transferred into everyday life. According to SportMatters.ca, when kids take home these values and share them with the family, a healthier lifestyle in family members is encouraged as well.

Youth sports teach the important lessons of teamwork, which can be applied to all areas of life on and off the playing field. Playing a sport will teach your child about goal setting, motivation, and working to accomplish something. Youth sports will also teach your child how to deal with defeat. It's not about winning; it's about trying hard, doing the best you can, and having fun. Those are all ideals that even as adults we lose sight of too readily.

Team building allows kids to get to know one another and build relationships, and teaches them how to develop social skills in a healthy, active environment. Many jobs require that employees work as teams to achieve tasks, and youth sports are similar. Playing sports as a child teaches teamwork, which will help the child as they get older in the workforce. Later in life, workers who participated in sports as kids are more likely to work ethically in their careers.

10 FACTORS TO CONSIDER WHEN CHOOSING A YOUTH LEAGUE

1. **Location** – Distance from home, school, work, league boundaries, etc.
2. **Travel** – Transportation, gas, food, lodging, carpooling, supervision, etc.
3. **Time** – Game and practice schedules, school and other commitments, parent involvement, etc.
4. **Costs** – Fees, uniforms, fundraising, additional instruction, snacks, etc.
5. **Type of Play** – Recreation verses competitive, rules, level of play, player rotation, etc.
6. **Safety** – Rules, equipment, condition of fields, pitching limitations, etc.
7. **Quality of Instruction** – Coaches' training, ability to teach skills and work with children.
8. **Leadership** – How decisions are made, teams drafted, all-stars chosen, conflicts resolved, etc.

9. **Reputation** – Past history, references from other parents, etc.
10. **Will this program provide a positive experience for my child?** Build self-esteem, reinforce good values, create friendships, etc.

Young players need more skill-based, fun-resulting experiences as opposed to high-pressurized organized league play.

At the middle school level, kids start dropping out of organized sports in big numbers. Some realize that a particular sport is just not for them, or they have the good sense to know that they simply do not have the talent to make it to the collegiate scholarship level, and they have the maturity to pursue another route to their future success. This is a critical time when tens of thousands of "late bloomers" quit playing sports altogether, and when millions of young Americans need to stay physically active.

The kids who have too much thrown at them too fast are the ones who are overwhelmed and most likely to give up. They lose their love for the game and the desire to get better on their own, but one of the reasons youth sports exist is to promote talent. If 70 percent of the kids who start out playing sports quit before puberty and before reaching their potential physical growth, millions of kids leave sports before they or anyone else recognize their true potential. As a result of this early burnout, college and professional sports are being deprived of talent.

The emphasis on winning and the consequences of selecting and playing "the best" during the early years neglects thousands of kids who would otherwise continue playing and developing into elite level athletes. This, in turn, has an adverse effect on the talent pool of American kids who might have been available to the collegiate and professional ranks.

PART III

THE COACH

What is a coach?

In the fourteenth century, a coach was a wheeled conveyance, usually pulled by a horse, used to take people where they wanted to go. Over time, that wheeled conveyance has changed to airplanes, trains, and automobiles. The definition of coach has also expanded to include individuals that give instruction and examples of how to do a variety of things, including sports and careers. In essence, attempting to take the athletes to where they want to go.

A successful coach must determine what the player's goals are, then adapt their coaching technique to align with the goals of the individual, rather than expecting players to adjust to the coach.

Addressing playing time, a player has to believe what he is told by his coach. Are you going to get your share of playing time? Are you told up front what your role is on the team?

Coaching qualifications are important. Knowledge of the sport is very important. Is winning the most important thing? Everyone wants to win, but how you accept winning and losing is important as well. Does a coach have the player's best interest in mind? Does he use pitch counts and proper rest for pitchers? Do they warm players up properly? Will they make every effort to help a player get to the next level? Is respect for authority and country a part of the team repertoire? Is the coach a good role model?

A quote from William Arthur ward lists four degrees of teachers: *"The mediocre teacher tells. The good teacher explains. The superior teacher demonstrates. The great teacher inspires."*

A coach is, in essence, a teacher, thus the quote can be applied to coaches as well. What are the general traits of these four levels?

- **The Mediocre Coach:** This individual is primarily a lecturer. He will generally explain things in detail. They may have a deep knowledge of the subject matter, but they present it basically through words.
- **The Good Coach:** This individual will take the time to present examples, written documentation, or photos to put the subject matter into easily understood language that the student will be able to apply.
- **The Superior Coach:** This person will demonstrate how the subject matter is accomplished by actually

doing the physical activity or having a trained assistant demonstrate.

- **The Great Coach:** This person will do all three of the above and, at the same time, create a learning environment that makes the student anxious to learn more. Basically, this individual makes learning fun and inspires the student to push themselves to the best of their ability.

  Great coaches are those who can teach and manage the game and, at the same time, understand the emotional and social development of kids. Great coaches exhibit class, honor, and integrity, and teach life skills. Finding one or more in some communities is sometimes a major challenge.

When coaches get too intense during a game, they tend to inflame their players, the spectators, and parents, thus disrupting the games, and causing chaos in the programs. Such unmannerly behavior from a coach can set a bad example for the players. Be polite. Coaches: Don't come running out onto the field with guns blazing, no matter how right you think you are. Parents: Stop yelling as you try to climb the chain link fence. An umpire wants—and needs—law and order, not the wild, wild west. You should want that, too.

Laugh. Be willing to laugh at the crazy things that happen on the field. Umpires are there to do a job, but they want to enjoy it, too. Having fun is what the game is about. Having a sense of humor shows the umpire that your priorities are straight.

Do the kids on your team regularly receive praise from you, and are they encouraged to continue to help the team? Cursing, obscene language or gestures, malicious or personal remarks to opponents should not be tolerated at any time by the coaching staff or the players. The players should spend their energies toward encouraging their teammates, and coaches should abstain from any personal action that might arouse unsportsmanlike behavior from players or spectators.

Coaches should expect from the officials a courteous and dignified attitude toward players and themselves. At the same time, coaches should confine their discussion with the game officials to the interpretations of the rules, and not constantly challenge umpire decisions involving judgment.

Coaches should teach their players to respect the dignity of the game, officials, the organizations which they represent, and the opponents. It is the duty of the coach to be in control of his players at all times in order to prevent any unsportsmanlike action toward opponents, officials, or spectators.

Along with taking breaks, coaches who vary practice routines are far less likely to experience a high rate of youth sports burnout. Rather than doing the same drills in the same order the same way every day, think about the ways you can change these routines as often as possible. Try to think of ways to coach kids that get them excited about being a part of the team, and you will see their enthusiasm and motivation increase. When practices are dull, predictable, and too consumed with instruction, kids are more likely to become stale and burned out.

Mentoring young men and women and helping a player perform is what coaching is all about. When you take on the position of coaching, whether you realize it or not, whether you want it or not, you are going to become a role model. What kind of impression will you leave on your players? Is it going to be a good impression or a bad one? You have a chance, usually reserved for parents, family members, and teachers, to leave a positive impact on your players. You need to ask yourself, what is important for you to pass along and how would you like to be viewed by your players and their parents?

The Positive Coaching Alliance has an outstanding training program, stressing one very important rule above all others: Professional sports are entertainment while youth sports are intended to be educational. Youth sports should not be focused on winning but on building the character and fundamental knowledge of the participants. Coaches should be trained to concentrate on instruction of the fundamentals over the glory of winning.

A lot of people know how to play the game and demonstrate how to play, but they do not know how to impart that knowledge to kids in a caring, non-brutal manner—keeping the fun in fundamentals. Too many amateur athletic coaches are so focused on winning that they fail to properly communicate with the younger, inexperienced kids.

If you are a coach, you should ask yourself on a daily basis if the kids you coach are having fun, and if the answer is no, think about how you might make the experience more enjoyable. Many coaches fail to realize that the average young person has a somewhat short attention span. When kids view youth sports as a job, you can be sure they will lose their interest, motivation, and excitement to play their best, and you will lose them.

Enjoying your experience with your players, as well as the players enjoying their experience with you, should be your first goal in coaching. Along with a good rapport, the ultimate goal is to see the players improve their skills in the game and to have their desire to play continue to grow.

A coach who thinks he knows it all is limited in his abilities. It doesn't matter if you have been a coach for 10 days or 10 years, you can still learn more about the nuances of the game. It requires an open mind and an observant eye. You will be surprised how often something happens, and you ask yourself how did that happen? Reconstruct and analyze the play and, surprise!

An insensitive coach can destroy a young person's self-esteem and make them feel as if they are not good enough to be on the same planet as anyone else, whereas a good coach can give a kid the encouragement necessary to meet any challenge life throws at them. Mistakes happen. When they happen, correct the problem, not the kid. If it happens once in a while, it is a mistake. If it happens constantly, it is a bad habit that must be corrected sometimes by several sessions of practice.

Generally, coaches in school-based programs have received some training in the psychological necessities of sports, but they have limited knowledge and/or experience in the sport. Occasionally, some of these people will have ego problems that get in their way.

When players are failing on the field striking out, dropping the baseball, or making wild throws, it is difficult for them to enjoy that experience and to develop confidence and self-esteem. Children who feel competent about their physical abilities have been found to more often participate and persist in physical activity whereas children who do not have that sense of competence are more likely to not become involved or to discontinue involvement. Thus, helping children to feel competent is seen as critical for sport participation and involvement.

Many young ball players have a variety of fears to overcome. Coaches cannot get frustrated and quit on the kids. Since young players have somewhat fragile egos, a good coach will work with a weak player to give him the confidence to grow and create a comfortable learning environment. This same coach will also work with and encourage the strong players to sharpen their skills. An impatient coach will often yell at them to the point that they feel incompetent or inferior simply because they are acting their age.

Probably the most common fear for young players is the fear of the ball at high speeds, high velocity pitches or hard-hit ground balls in particular. Fear of the ball at bat can only be overcome by boosting the kid's confidence and making him hungry to hit. Have them run through their basic mechanics while waiting for the pitch and then go after the first pitch, no matter where it is. After they beat their fear, they can start learning to be selective at bat.

Hard hit ground balls cause alarm in a lot of experienced players as well. The survival instinct tells us to bail or to get out of the way, an instinct we have to overcome. Fielding several hard-hit balls is the only way to beat this phobia. One thing that can help is to have the player wear a catcher's helmet and a small chest protector until they are comfortable staying down and in front of the ball, and concentrating on the mechanics of fielding.

Occasionally, a coach will have a challenge where a kid has a medical problem or some type of debilitating injury from an early age that makes learning a problem. I had one young man who had suffered a brain injury at a young age, and he had trouble following my leads on certain physical movements. We were both right-handed and when I would face him and show him how to move his feet or arms, he would try to move as a left hander. I realized it was as if he was looking at a mirror, so I turned around and had him observe from behind. Then he got the point.

TRAITS OF A GOOD COACH

- A quality coach can teach players how to play the game and to develop character, confidence, and self-esteem.
- A good coach is basically supportive of the kids, and he is patient when correcting learned bad habits.
- He will de-emphasize winning and focus on the rules, learning the fundamentals, and having fun.
- He keeps his temper and doesn't yell at players, game officials, or other coaches.
- He keeps discipline a matter between coach and player and does not embarrass the kids in front of the team or the crowd.
- He praises good performance but does not criticize a player for mistakes.
- He places a player's health and welfare ahead of winning.

TRAITS OF A BAD COACH:

- A bad coach puts his personal goals ahead of the kids.
- He uses the carrot on a stick system of reward if you win; punish if you lose.

- He believes in a win-at-all-costs philosophy. If the team is not winning, the inexperienced kids will not get much, if any, playing time.
- He encourages disrespectful attitudes toward the opposition.
- If a kid makes a mistake in the field, he allows the team members to get on the kid instead of encouraging them to get behind the kid.

THE PROBLEM WITH TRAVEL BALL

> *"I have always felt that youngsters learn the game best in an unstructured setting. An organized game structure does not allow kids to experiment with different things. Youngsters might want to switch-hit, or maybe try a different position, or change their batting stance or the way they pitch a ball—all things they could do easily in a pickup game. That type of experimentation isn't really encouraged during the course of a formal game, and kids miss out. Experimenting is great fun for kids. It allows them to be, well, kids."*
>
> – Cal Ripken, Jr.

The fundamentals must be practiced continually, even at the big-league level. Travel baseball forces kids to fully dedicate their time, energy, and interest into one activity. This is not natural in the early stages of life. Basically, what travel baseball has done is put eight to 11 year olds in an adult created setting where the pressure to win and perform takes precedent over the emotional and athletic development of the players themselves.

> *"Many kids have missed out on the simple pleasure of playing catch with a parent or sibling. Since they are not playing enough catch, the throwing skills of young children have diminished. They need to make playing catch fun and challenging. Young players need more skill-based, fun-resulting experiences, as opposed to high-pressurized organized league play."*
>
> – Don Weiskopf, publisher of *Baseball Play America*

Pick-up games and just "playing for fun" should be encouraged. The key at this vulnerable stage is to keep them playing the sports they enjoy—if not on school or youth teams, then informally with friends. On those days when there are not enough kids to make two teams, other games can be utilized to keep the spirits up. Kids can play Workup, where two or three batters hit until they are put out. After the put out, that hitter goes to Right Field and works his way back up to the plate, progressing to center field, to left field, around the infield to pitcher and catcher, then another shot at bat. Fewer than eight or nine kids means they can play 500. One kid hits the ball to the others spaced across the outfield, and points are assigned for fly balls, one hoppers, or grounders. The first one to reach 500 points replaces the batter and the game continues.

When there are too many games, there isn't enough time for practice and the proper development of fundamental skills. An organized game structure does not allow kids to experiment with different approaches. Youngsters might want to switch-hit, or maybe try a different position, or change their batting stance or the way they pitch a ball—all things they could do easily in a pickup game. That type of experimentation isn't really encouraged during the course of a formal game, and kids miss out. Experimenting is great fun for kids. It allows them to be kids.

The potential for athletic excellence and success cannot always be identified at an early age, and inferior athletes will frequently blossom and attain success in later years given the right opportunity to compete and develop their skills. Rather than winning, the focus for youth baseball needs to be on development. After all, once these kids hit puberty, it is really not going to matter which travel team your son played on and how many tournaments they won. Consistent practice time is a critical component to this development.

Early specialization has been related to an increase in burnout or withdrawal from sport as a result of chronic stress. Burnout results many times from participation in too many sports, including having a child play in numerous leagues in order to specialize their talents, often leading to physical harm. This latter scenario may pose the greatest danger for the player.

Unfortunately, the quest for tournaments has taken a serious toll on summer baseball. August has gone to fishing and picnic season, and these valuable summer baseball opportunities have been lost. Sandlots are now mostly empty around the country. A state championship is the highest honor in high school ball, so why is a national championship necessary for kids not even in high school?

According to the National Alliance for Sports and the Youth Sports Institute at Michigan State reports, 70 percent of these kids quit playing league sports by age 13—and never play them again. Playing sports loses its enjoyment for them, and fun takes a back seat to winning.

The Youth Sports Institute at Michigan State listed the top ten reasons why kids quit:

1. They lost interest;
2. They were not having fun;
3. It required too much time;
4. The coach played favorites;
5. The coach was a poor teacher;
6. They got tired of playing;
7. Too much emphasis on winning;
8. They wanted to participate in other non-sport activities;

9. They needed more time to study;
10. There was too much pressure.

With the arrival of travel ball programs, a somewhat different breed of coach has emerged. Although there are some very qualified individuals in these programs, there are those who are there only to satisfy their own egos, trying to vicariously live out fantasies of their youth or to simply try and push their own children to the highest level at any cost.

Many of these individuals have had no training or experience, but they have developed a strong dislike for the way the programs they were involved with were being operated. These are the coaches who carry themselves with an air of superiority supported by an attitude of "I know what is best!" They look and dress the part with $100 sunglasses and custom-made paraphernalia, but most travel coaches possess as much knowledge as your average local league coach, maybe less. They will act as if they are managing professional players, but there is no sign of professionalism when they throwing the equipment, arguing with officials, and sulking after losses, trying to find someone else to blame. These are the guys who can seriously damage your kids, physically and emotionally.

Game situations tend to restrict kids. Youngsters don't want to make a mistake in a real game, so they become much more tentative in their play. They won't try something new because they're afraid that they may fail and suffer a tongue-lashing from their coach, their teammates, or possibly even their mom or dad. How in the world is a young ballplayer going to develop his skills at unless he gets the chance to go out and experiment and push his limits every so often?

PART IV

THE FOUR ROLES OF SPORTS PARTICPATION

Since the inception of youth sports programs, the biggest problem has been "roles." Common sense and a true sense of "reality" led to the creation and definition of the four roles of youth sports. This little rule clearly outlines that every person involved in youth games has one role only. When attending a youth contest, each person must make a conscious decision as to what their role is and maintain JUST that role throughout the entire game.

The Four Roles are:

1. If you are a **PLAYER – JUST** play the game and have FUN! Live clean and play hard. Play for the love of the game, winning without boasting, losing without excuse, but never quitting. Respect officials and accept their decisions, and

never forget that when people judge a player's actions, they judge not only the player, but the team, the league, and the community the player represents.

2. If you are the **UMPIRE or REFEREE – JUST** know the rules and call the game fairly. Know the rules, be fair and firm in all decisions, and call them as you see them. Treat players and managers and coaches courteously and demand the same treatment for yourselves. Know the game is for the players, and let the players have the spotlight. Once in a while, you will run across an official who refuses to bend. He will not listen to a request that maybe his field partner may have had a better angle on a play, and his pride will not allow him to change a call.
3. If you are a **COACH – JUST** coach and leave the officiating to the men with the striped shirts. Inspire in the players a love for the game and a desire to win, teaching that it is better to lose fairly than to win unfairly. Teach players and spectators to respect officials by setting a good example. Be the type of person you want the players to be. One thing is certain about baseball: No matter how much you think you know about the game or coaching, you can always learn something new if you just pay attention and admit that you don't know everything.
4. If you are a **FAN, PARENT, ETC. – JUST** watch the game and be positive for all the players! Never boo officials or

> players or managers or coaches. Parents, you must be willing to give up the responsibility of your children to the coach during the game, and everyone must appreciate a good play, no matter who makes it. Know that your community gets the blame—or the praise—for your conduct and recognize the need for more sportsmen and fewer "sports." If you have a problem with the coach, address it one on one in private and not in front of players or other spectators. Be an adult.

Parents tend to have the best interests in mind for their children. However, parents and coaches can place a great amount of pressure on their children to excel in sports. This form of pressure often translates into the child training and practicing for his/her sport year-round. Most problems in youth sports are from people older than 18 who are setting bad examples of sportsmanship, instilling a win-first attitude to youth, and applying professional sports development models and programs to youth sports.

Parents should be encouraged to share with their children and to realize that this is a child's game, and it will go on, even if your child does not have a particularly great day. If your child or a teammate has an off day at practice or doesn't perform well in a game, big deal. Forget about the negatives. Pick out one or two positive things and really get excited about them. This will pick the player up and get him excited about going back on the field and trying again.

Spend time talking with your kids after the game and get their view on how it went. This is a great time for bonding with your kids. Remember that a game of catch is another great tool for bonding; conversation just comes naturally.

Too many parents believe that it is their right and "job" to do everything in order for their child to win. It seems that these parents cannot grasp the fact that sports games are structured for child development, which unfortunately includes learning to lose with dignity and determination, and not the accumulation of trophies. During the game, stay seated in the bleachers. Do not yell to the children about how to play or about what they are doing wrong.

As a parent you want your kids to succeed at everything they do, and sometimes, it's hard. Cal Ripken, says you, as a parent and a coach, have to understand, you have to act like you know what's going to happen. And when something good happens, you've got to stay here. When something bad happens, you've got to stay here.

Mr. Ripken also believes that there is a danger of cheering too much; and a danger in what can happen in a baseball game when one 10-year-old team is out there beating up another 10-year-old team, and the parents are on the side, high-fiving, cheering, and carrying on. Number one, that has a negative effect on the 10-year-old kids who are getting beaten. But sometimes, the game can turn completely around. The earlier "beaten team" may come back to win, and all the earlier cheering on the side that was winning turns to dead silence, and now those kids from the team that gets beat actually thinks they did something wrong.

Parents should be involved, but not intensely consumed with their child's activity—basically, be a good sports spectator. Simply put, let the "kids be kids," and empower them to have FUN while they learn the lessons of the sport, which in turn will teach them to be good, productive citizens. Allow them to learn the lessons that the games have to teach. Their childhood will soon be gone, and they will move on, so enjoy the time you have with them while you have it.

PART V

PASSION FOR THE GAME

"Champions Aren't made in the gyms. Champions are made from something they have deep inside them – a desire, a dream, a vision."

– Muhammad Ali

Passion for the game is the burning desire to be the best you can be and to focus at the task on hand. This means giving things up to accomplish a goal and to put "your all" into achieving personal and team success. That is true passion. Ty Cobb was probably the most ferocious man to ever play the game, but regardless of the bad reputation that was heaped on him, he believed that the sun rose and set in baseball. Cobb wanted to be a doctor, but he couldn't spend the time with his education and still play baseball.

Good players are developed, not born, so if a player has the tools and an aggressive attitude, they have a good chance to develop into a quality player. Remember, anyone can improve over time, even athletic ability, if the player is inspired and willing to put forth the effort.

When I was 10 years old, our coach announced that the team would only use one 10-year-old pitcher. I was matched against another boy, and I lost. I was furious but determined that I would be there next year. During the winter, I worked hard at conditioning—lots of pushups and pull ups and building up the strength in my wrists and forearms. I used a tool made from a piece of broken broomstick with a hole drilled through to accommodate a length of rope tied to a boat anchor. I would hold the tool straight out from my body and roll the handle to raise and lower the weight. By the next spring, in addition to a growth spurt of four or five inches, I was able to beat out the two 12-year-olds on the team and became the starting pitcher. I do regret that I knew nothing of inventions and so forth, because now there is a tool of the same basic design on the market as I used.

Kids mature at different rates physically, emotionally, and in terms of their motor skills. The emphasis on winning and the consequences of selecting and playing "the best" during the early years neglects thousands of kids who would otherwise continue playing and developing into elite level athletes. Late bloomers are being denied the opportunity to play unless the team is fortunate enough to have a coach who can see potential in the smaller, young boy. With proper nurturing, given a chance to build a strong foundation in the fundamentals at this younger, less athletic age, inferior athletes will frequently blossom and attain success in later years given the right opportunity to compete and develop their skills.

Do your players exhibit true passion? In any youth sports program, the emphasis should be on the proper instruction of the fundamentals over winning, keeping the fun in fundamentals and developing a passion for the game. Many say they want to play baseball and are passionate about it, BUT they will not do the work nor dedicate themselves to be the best they can be, win or lose.

Ty Cobb studied the other players of every team, looking for their weaknesses. When he found such a weakness, he would exploit it to the max, many times getting him more "bad boy" points. He did, however, like kids and wanted them to grow up decent. He believed that baseball was the best solution to a lot of juvenile problems. In the words of the great Ty Cobb: *"Teach a kid to throw a baseball and he won't throw a rock."*

Unfortunately, not every kid can play high school baseball and only about 10 percent of high school ballplayers move on to play in college. If you're having hopes of your son being the next multi-million-dollar big leaguer, understand that only about 1 percent of high school players will even have a slim chance to step on the field as a professional. So please, don't place too much pressure on your child by telling everyone he's going to be the next Derek Jeter or Clayton Kershaw. Chances are, he's already pressuring himself enough as it is. Here is a simple checklist to see if your 10- to 12-year-old is on track to becoming a very good ballplayer, possibly en route to playing high school or college baseball:

- They can throw and catch with ease, rarely dropping the ball or throwing it away while playing catch.
- Hitting live pitching to all fields is not a problem.
- They field ground balls in a smooth manner with soft hands.
- Throws from the left side of the infield to first base are starting to level out with only a slight arc.
- As a pitcher, they can consistently throw the ball to the glove and not just get the ball over the plate.
- They understand the rules of the game and at times show certain instincts as a player.

SIX QUALITIES OF A WINNING ATHLETE

- A willingness to take coaching and study the game.
- A spirit of competition in practice as well as in games.
- An intense desire to win and the ability to gracefully accept a loss.

- A willingness to practice hard at all times.
- A willingness to make personal sacrifices for the good of the team.
- A strong desire to improve themselves on and off the field

To be the best in the world (in any field), young players must participate and practice more than just about everybody. It is hard to develop a fundamental skill without practicing it over and over. Teaching fundamentals from a team and an individual standpoint is difficult during games. The excitement and pressure surrounding an organized game is not an environment conducive to teaching successfully.

Sitting on the bench and learning how to support teammates from the sidelines is a valuable lesson that all kids should learn. Too many kids, especially the more advanced players, rarely, if ever, spend much time on the bench. As a result of this early spoiling, some high school coaches are having to deal with incoming freshman with bad attitudes and a strong sense of entitlement.

Consistent practice time is a critical component to this development. Practice is extremely important for developing the fundamental skills necessary for players to be successful as they continue climbing the youth baseball ladder. Practice also is essential for teaching team fundamentals and allowing players to learn about the nuances of the game.

The key to developing expertise in the fundamental skills lies in learning and remembering the basic mechanics involved. Players in any sport need to keep in mind that they are human, and perfection is not a human trait. If they believe they can be perfect, they will only be perfectly disappointed. Contrary to popular belief, the old adage "practice makes perfect" is not true. Vince Lombardi, coach of the Green Bay Packers, stated it best.

> *"Gentlemen, we will chase perfection, and we will chase it relentlessly, knowing all the while we can never attain it. But along the way, we shall catch excellence."*
>
> – Vince Lombardi

PART VI

LEARNING FROM THE BENCH

Everybody should, at one time or another, experience "bench time." "Dugout Skills" refer to the mental skills exercised in the dugout during these times. These will increase and improve your game as well as help your teammates gain focus and insight into the game at hand while keeping your head in the game. Players who pay attention during the game are those who will improve at a greater rate and will become valuable assets to their coach and team. You should learn from every pitch and situation. Study the umpire, the pitcher, the defense...and take the advantage!

WATCH THE UMPIRE

- Does he consistently call a high or low strike?
- Does he have a big or small strike zone? Does he set up the same for every pitch?

- Is he consistent with the inside/outside pitch?
- Does he change his calls depending on the score? The inning?

WATCH THE PITCHER/TEAM DEFENSE

- How are they set up? Outfield too deep or too shallow?
- Any advantages for your team? Gaps in the outfield?
- Does the defense shift with the pitches or change according to the count?
- Do the infielders creep to the plate? Are they standing flat footed?
- Do they hit the cutoffs? Cover their bases? Do they back up throws and plays?

PART VII

THE OFFENSE

The offense mostly consists of hitting and running. Plenty of hustle and spirit and an attitude of confidence play an important role in a strong offense. Speed and quickness on the base paths and aggressive base running will open up opportunities for a number of offensive tactics.

HITTING

Hitting will involve a proper stance, a level swing, and bunting. To be a successful hitter, know there is a big difference between a "batter" and a "hitter." A hitter with an aggressive swing, who is confident and believes in his abilities, can lift the entire team with just his presence, whereas a batter, a doubtful hitter, lends nothing to the team. Pitchers will try to intimidate hitters, but the confident hitter will many times reverse the situation.

The first rule of hitting is to have a clear understanding that the purpose of hitting is to hit the ball hard every time, to hit line drives, hard ground balls, and to be mentally ready to hit every pitch in every at bat. Never waste a time at bat because at bats are precious.

Are you a hitter or are you just a batter? A batter is more like a tourist; he is just there to look and see what the pitcher is about. A properly prepared hitter knows what he wants and is prepared for it on every pitch. He starts his routine the same and, if fooled, can adjust to at least foul the ball away, forcing the pitcher to throw more pitches and increasing the chance for a mistake.

A good hitter learns how to hit behind the runner, hitting to the opposite field, which is essential in a successful hit and run. When teams apply a "shift" in the defense, they will leave gaps on one side of the field. Ty Cobb believed that Ted Williams could have had a lot more hits if he would have gone to the opposite field when the defense put a "shift" on him.

The second, and maybe most important rule is: Always believe that you can do it! Knowing this, you may fail at times, but you must believe in yourself. Remember, even the best professionals fail seven out of 10 times.

Ty Cobb was believed to be the most aggressive hitter in the game. When questioned about his style, Cobb was quoted on his intimidating methods toward pitchers thus: "*Every great batter works on the theory that the pitcher is more afraid of him than he is of the pitcher."*

Learn to read the pitcher. Pick up the ball at the pitchers' release point and cue the pitcher's action to tip pitches by noting various habits he has developed. Ty Cobb studied the great Walter Johnson and realized that Johnson had a certain "phobia," as it were, about hitting a batter. Using this knowledge, Cobb would crowd the plate, causing Johnson to throw outside, which allowed Cobb to slap the ball to the opposite field for hits.

Develop a hitting specific routine prior to the at bat in the dugout and on-deck circle. Think about and assess the situation before stepping into the batter's box. Relax and take deep breaths as you dig in (get oxygen to the brain and muscles). Exhale fully before addressing the pitcher.

Maximize your performance by utilizing the "percentage" system of baseball rather than guess hitting, by making wise, tactical hitting decisions based on the following factors:

- Location in the batter's box;
- Anticipate pitch based on the count;
- Offensive situation;
- Playing field conditions.

Step out after every pitch, breathe deep, focus on your mechanics. No matter what the count, always expect a fastball. Adjust to the off-speed pitch accordingly. If you are fooled by a pitch, throw your hands at the ball and try to slap it to the opposite field or foul it off.

Move up in the box in the bunt situation; back in the box for the hit and run situation.

Some coaches will insist, but there is no standard batting stance. Stan Musial said that although many kids tried to mimic his stance and style, they should adapt to what is comfortable to them, no matter what the books and "specialists" say. The most important point is that the hitter is comfortable, with the feet spread slightly, but the hitter must have his weight on the back foot when he starts his swing for maximum power. Too many hitters spread their feet too far and thus their weight does not transfer when needed.

The stride can be as much as 12 to 18 inches, or it can be nothing more than turning the foot on the heel of the front foot.

The head stays down, the front shoulder leads toward the pitch, and the eyes stay fixed on the ball until the point of contact. At the point of contact, the wrists will roll over for a smooth and thorough follow through.

The hands should be positioned at the top of the strike zone to minimize the up and down travel of the hands. The hands should travel straight back and then forward, never up and down If the hands are too high or too low, it is difficult to get a level cut. When the bat travels up or down during the swing, the front shoulder is pulled or pushed away from the ball, and the chances of connecting with the ball is tough.

Remember, a bad habit is hard to correct. Beginners should concentrate on a level swing at all times. When they reach the high school level, situations come up where a ground ball or a fly ball may be necessary. When they reach that level, a good coach can show them how to cut down on the ball for a ground ball and to uppercut slightly for the fly ball.

A lot of young players will go to a batting cage and hit the ball pretty good, and then freeze up when facing a live pitcher. The reason is that the batting cage is a controlled situation where there is no guesswork as to where the pitch is coming and whether it will be a strike or not. Live pitchers can alter the speed, location, and break of the ball, so the novice will hesitate, throwing off his timing. The only remedy for this is live pitching, whether it is in a game, a practice or during a non-stress fun game.

BUNTING

The bunt is an excellent tool for moving a runner into scoring position or avoiding a double play. Applied at the correct time, it can draw in a defense and open a possible hole for a base hit. The bunt is possibly the most unpredictable action in baseball.

It can be the most boring moment of the game, or it can be the most exciting play in the game, depending on when it occurs.

A sound bunting game and squeeze plays can be the difference between a "ho-hum" game and an "Oh my!" game. When it is used to simply move the runner over one base, and everybody in the ballpark expects it, it is just a matter of the hitter getting the ball down right. This is a good time to go to the concession stand.

When used in conjunction with a runner stealing in a run and bunt play or a suicide squeeze play, the bunt is certain to get the crowd to their feet and buzzing with enthusiasm.

When bunting, the batter is actually catching the ball with the bat. The bat is considered an extension of the batter's arm, and the ball is "caught" with basically the same action as when playing catch—a slight "give" of the hands. The bat is not gripped tightly; the knees are bent slightly, and the bat is held out in front of the plate six to 12 inches. If the bat is gripped too tight, the impact of the ball is too hard, and the ball travels too far, sometimes creating an easy play for the defense.

Always start with the bat at the top of the strike zone. By moving down on the ball, there is less chance of a pop up. If you have to raise your hands, the pitch is too high. Unless there is a squeeze play on, take the pitch and make the pitcher throw another.

The direction of the bunt is determined by the angle of the bat. To bunt down the third base line, the hitter will push the head of the bat toward the pitcher while pulling the handle back toward the catcher. To guide the ball to the right side, the handle is pushed toward the pitcher and the head is pulled toward the catcher.

Once in a while, the batter can deploy a "jack bunt" or "push bunt" to move the runner(s) and possibly get an infield base hit. With this maneuver, a tight grip can be used to the offensive team's advantage. With an aggressive defense charging hard, the batter will push the ball rather than catch it, the intention being to move the ball past the pitcher into the hole vacated by the second baseman moving to cover first base.

THE RUNNING GAME

A successful running game will employ leading off, getting a jump, stealing bases, cutting the corners of the bases, and sliding. While basic speed is important, quickness and reading the defense are critical to success. A runner that gets a lead but is slow to get the jump will usually get thrown out.

Aggressive base running starts with all-out hustle to first base, and rounding first base with possibilities of going to second base on base hits to the outfield. Delayed and double steals and the run and hit are tools that can keep a defense guessing and open up opportunities for the hitters.

An alert runner should be able to get a minimum lead of three to four strides. By taking a "one way" lead (anticipating a throw to the base and planning to go back), the runner can study the pitcher to see what he does when he makes his move to the base or to deliver to the plate. A right-handed pitcher will have to move his left foot or left hip toward first base in order to throw to the base. If the foot moves any other direction, he is going to the plate (with the exception of stepping back with the right foot to disengage the rubber). Once the runner has determined what to watch for, he can extend the lead slightly and be ready to break at the first move.

Leading off from second base is slightly more complicated since there are two fielders working together to keep the runner close. Usually, the third base coach watches the shortstop and the runner watches the pitcher while watching the movements of the second baseman from the corner of the eye.

Some coaches want their runners to move away from the baseline toward the shortstop. They believe that this will give them an advantage over the shortstops' movements, but in reality, it simply adds two to four extra strides to the distance to third base. A better move is to take a step toward the pitcher with each step off the base. This gives the pitcher a distorted view that looks like the runner is closer to second base than he is.

When breaking for the next base, the runner should always start with a "crossover" step (leading with the left foot). This gives the runner a full stride and allows him to get to full speed within three or four strides. Throwing the right elbow toward the next base will help put the body in motion to lead with the crossover step.

Cutting the inside corner of the bases will shorten the distance between bases by cutting down the number of strides necessary. Approximately eight to 10 feet from the base, the runner makes a short detour to the right, which will allow him to cut the corner at a direct angle toward the next base.

SLIDING

The slide can be smooth or dangerously clumsy. It should be practiced on grass or sand. Too many young players are not taught proper sliding technique, so they resort to a headfirst slide. There is no time savings in a headfirst slide, but the danger of serious injury is amplified four ways:

1. A face-first slide takes the runner directly at the base with no options to avoid a tag.
2. A finger or wrist could easily be broken from contact with the fielder or the base.
3. A good throw from the catcher could hit the runner in the head.
4. A collision with the fielder could result in injuries to both players.

There are several slides that can be effective and safe while providing a means to slide around the tag. Three of the most often used are:

1. The "Pop Up" slide gives the runner an option to slide under the tag and the ability to immediately get up and go to the next base.
2. The "Hook Slide" allows the option of sliding to the outside on either side of the base, and the fielder has a smaller target for the tag.
3. The "By-Pass" slide allows the runner to slide by the fielder and reach behind the fielder for the back side of the base.

PART VIII

THE DEFENSE

The basic responsibility of the defense is to keep runners off the bases. The pitcher should try to keep the hitters from getting a solid hit. A pitcher who has no control will walk too many batters or get beaten by the hitters. A good pitcher will allow a minimum of two or three walks in a nine-inning game.

Should a hitter get on base, there are basically three options to remove him—a pick off, catch the runner stealing, or a double-play ground ball.

Mental preparation and awareness are what makes a successful defense. Every player should be prepared for the ball to come to them on every play and know what to do depending on the situation. If a player is not directly involved with the play, they should anticipate where the play will go and be prepared to back up any throws involved with the play. When you watch a well-coached team, you will see the outfielders moving into position on every hit ball, sometimes to make a play, but most times to back up a play in case of a miscue.

A team with weak defense is in serious trouble! Without a stout defense, the offense cannot afford to have a bad day or the game is lost. A good defense should be strong up the middle (catcher, second base, shortstop, and center field). How well these players perform will provide the confidence needed by the offense, the pitcher, and the other four positions. A sharp defense may utilize a number of defensive tactics, but I have only mentioned some of the most common plays below.

Everything in defense revolves around being able to catch and throw the ball. It serves no purpose in trying to master a complicated play before learning to catch and throw properly; a team can't expect to execute a double-play when one guy can't throw the ball and the other one can't catch it. Players should spend most of their time on catching and throwing because without those skills defensive play will always be inconsistent.

Throwing is a lost art. Throwing isn't something that we should do "just" to get our arms loose. Throwing should be done to maximize that skill; to develop it like any other skill to become a strength rather than a potential weakness. Weak and lazy throws from the outfield or high "rainbow" throws allow runners extra time to advance. Every throw should be hard and direct.

Playing catch should be done to improve the player's ability, not just to warm up the arm. The key to improving the basic skills of catching and throwing the ball can be accomplished by using proper mechanics when warming up in practice.

1. Begin the catching-moving-throwing movement as the ball approaches to develop a proper and consistent rhythm, moving the feet to get to the ball rather than standing still and reaching, gripping the ball across the seams while taking the ball out of the glove.
2. When the ball is in the glove, players should begin to move the hands toward the throwing position and shift the feet simultaneously into the throwing position.
3. Players should practice the throwing skills that they will need in game action.
4. To develop consistent control, players should throw at a target on every throw. Control isn't just for pitchers.
5. Strengthen the arm in warm-up to develop arm strength by utilizing the long toss technique, gradually increasing the distance each day. Start the warm-up at a short distance and gradually lengthen the throws to that of the longest throw they must make during a game.

CATCHING

The position of catcher is one of the most important jobs on the baseball field. From his position, he is able to see every play developing, and that makes it his job to be the "traffic director" on the field. He will direct the defense for relays and cutoffs that many times cut off runners and foil the offensive play to get the team out of a tight spot.

A strong arm is useful, but a quick release is more important. When a runner strays too far off a base, a quick snap throw may catch and eliminate them. On a failed bunt attempt, a quick throw may catch a runner caught in trying to reverse his direction. A two-step release should be practiced and used at all times. As the catcher receives the ball, he should take a step with his right foot, one step with his left foot, and then make the throw to either third or second base.

The catcher is the defensive leader. He needs to know everything about every position. The catcher must catch or block every pitched ball (easier said than done). He has to decide when to let a throw come through or to cut the throw and attempt to make an out at another base sometimes allowing a run to score. He may get "roughed up" a bit on plays at the plate when he has to block the runner from scoring and make a tag.

He needs to know all the bunt plays, all of the relay situations, he has to call all of the defensive alignments, and occasionally, he has to be the steadying force for a nervous or rattled pitcher. He is the unsung hero when the team wins.

The catcher should receive pitches with the shoulders square to the incoming ball. Balls below the waist should be caught with the fingers facing down and balls above the waist with the fingers up. A good catcher will follow the ball into the glove with the throwing hand. Some coaches insist on the catcher keeping his throwing hand behind his back when receiving, catching the ball with one hand, but that will result in a delay of transferring the ball from the glove to the throwing hand. Not a big delay, but oftentimes, too much of a delay to throw the runner out stealing.

A catcher should receive the baseball with his elbow near his body, pointed down. Keeping the palm of his catching hand facing in, towards the center of the plate positions the catcher's body directly behind the baseball, which in turn keeps his arm from drifting out of the strike zone on inside or outside pitches. From this position, he can sometimes "frame" a pitch that is inside, as the glove position and movement toward the center of the plate will sometimes convince an umpire that the pitch is a strike.

Blocking can only be practiced with real bad tosses. Coaches should throw balls from a distance of 20 or 30 feet in the dirt in front of the catcher. The catcher should work on going down on both knees to block the ball and putting the top of the body over the ball, allowing the ball to bounce off the body or the chest protector. The head will be out over the ball, and the glove will be in between the knees to cover the hole there. A tennis ball is a safe way to work on blocks and not risk damaging a finger.

THE PITCHER

The umpire may say the words "play ball!" but everything begins with the pitcher. Each and every other play waits until the pitcher takes a windup or come set. The runners plan their moves, the hitters determine what the pitch might be, and the fielders await the pitch and remind themselves of what their part will be when the play develops. The pitch is delivered, and the game progresses. Many of those in the grandstand have no idea what the pitcher has gone through in preparation for that first pitch and what will follow.

PITCHING MECHANICS

The pitcher should have gone through a thorough warm-up in the bullpen to make sure his arm feels right, that the ball is moving as it should, his control is tip top and that all his repertoire of pitches is ready to go. He has made mental notes about some of the opposing hitters, so he can handle them. Sandy Koufax was known to throw 50 pitches or more in the bullpen until he felt "right" with his mechanics.

WHAT ARE SOME OF THE MOST BASIC MECHANICS?

On the windup, the pitcher should step straight back and deliver in a straight line with the catcher. The pitcher should move from a bent back leg to get lower, leading with the front hip and landing on flexed front leg in a straight line toward the plate. This movement is known as the "drop and drive."

The pitcher's stride must be long enough to complete his back leg drive before he lands. The back leg should be at nearly full extension just before landing. Always drive hard enough off the rubber so that the back leg naturally comes forward to a fielding position. For a baseball pitcher, the stride's length should depend on where he can best execute his hip and shoulder rotation. This will improve command of the baseball and maximize the ball movement and velocity. The stride is usually two thirds to three quarters of the player's height. Short stride kills velocity, throws off the timing, and adds stress to the arm.

Break the hands before the head and front hip have started to move away from the rubber, taking the ball out of the glove with fingers on top and thumb underneath, swinging the hand down, back, and up into the cocked position, being sure that the throwing arm gets back into a natural but fully-extended position.

The head should be positioned between the feet upon landing. The pitcher should land with his weight on the middle to inside of his landing foot (front knee positioned over his ankle) and not falling off to one side or the other. If not, speed and control is reduced, and stress is applied to the arm.

At ball release, the pitcher's head and chest should be positioned in line with and out over his landing knee. If the head is behind the landing knee, this indicates he is not creating enough forward momentum (not driving hard enough off the rubber).

Pitchers need to bend their front knee at foot strike to get their hips through the pitching zone correctly and to deliver a downward plane on all pitches. Landing on the heel of the front foot stops maximum, efficient rotation of the hips, and jars the execution of the pitch. The bent knee for pitchers will help them keep the ball down for more ground balls. Finish with the trunk flexed forward to a flat back position, not standing straight up (often referred to as finishing low).

The pitcher starts every play and tries to keep batters from reaching base safely. One of a pitchers' biggest obstacles is the base on balls, the walk. This one is solely on the pitcher and can cause the pitcher to doubt his ability. Some walks are given on close pitches that the pitcher is certain the pitch was a strike. At this point, it is imperative that the pitcher maintains his composure and avoids any emotional outburst. His job is to throw the pitch and accept the calls of the umpire.

Should a batter become a runner, the pitcher has a couple of options to remove those runners.

PREVENTING THE STOLEN BASE

Pitchers don't need to pick off runners to prevent base runners from stealing. Shortening the lead by a step or making the runner wait a half-second longer on his break will keep runners at bay and give the catcher a better chance to throw the runner out. This can be accomplished by varying the time between coming set and release, or sometimes by taking a second look at the runner before delivering.

The right-handed pitcher needs to work on two things: quick footwork and changing the timing in the set position. Changing the timing from the set position will help keep the runner from picking up a pattern and getting a good jump. A quick pitch, holding for differing lengths of time before delivering the pitch, stepping off the rubber after a few seconds and the slide step (delivering the ball without lifting the leg) will disrupt the runner's timing. The key is to be able to do this without losing the focus on the batter.

Along with the quick footwork, the pitcher needs to keep the throw to first short and quick as well, rather than throwing with the same motion they use to throw to the plate with a long arm motion.

PICK-OFF PLAYS

Runners reaching base can be erased by a pick-off throw to first base or by means of a pick off play between the pitcher and the middle infielders. The pick off to first base should be a quick, accurate throw to the inside corner of the bag three to six inches off the ground. This allows the first baseman to catch the ball and sweep tag the inside corner of the base as the runner slides or dives back in.

SECOND BASE PICK-OFF

There are two basic pick-off moves to second base: the daylight play or the count.

The daylight play basically means when the pitcher is in the set position, when he checks the runner and sees a daylight space between the shortstop and the runner, he turns and throws to the third base side of the bag (again three to six inches off the ground).

The count play works best on the runners who are more cautious with their lead. The second baseman, as a decoy, will bluff moves to the base, and the shortstop pretends to not be too interested in the runner's lead. As the pitcher comes set, the second baseman retreats from the base, and the pitcher will be watching the runner and the shortstop. When the pitcher's hands come set, he will turn his head toward the plate. At that moment, the pitcher and the shortstop start a count of two to three seconds (*one-thousand one, one-thousand two*). At the end of the second count, the fielder breaks hard for the base, and the pitcher turns and throws to the third base corner of the bag.

THE INFIELDERS

The primary responsibility of the infielders is to field ground balls and short pop flies and make accurate throws in time to put the batter or runner out.

The fielders should be alert at all times to the possible moves by the offense (stealing a base, bunt situations, etc.) and know in advance where the most likely play will be when the ball comes to them.

The shortstop and the second baseman work as a unit to keep the defense prepared. One of these players is many times the team captain and will position himself where they can see the signals from the catcher and pass along signals to the other fielders in order to position the defense.

Using their knowledge of the pitcher's ability and control, these two will signal each other where they anticipate the hitter will hit the ball and adjust the defense to make the necessary play. The signal used can be a simple hand or glove movement or an audible signal (a color, number, etc.).

The shortstop and/or second baseman will work with the catcher to line up the defense for relay throws to third base and home plate. A good relay system is a prominent feature of every successful team.

The third baseman has a responsibility to "guard the line," prevent successful bunts to the left side of the infield, and to cut off shallow ground balls between the mound and third base.

DEFENSE AGAINST FIRST AND THIRD SITUATIONS

With runners at first and third, the defense must have a plan for making the best plays to prevent a successful double steal, delayed steal, bunt, or hit & run.

Options:

A. Throw runner from first base out at second and prepare for a return throw if runner on third breaks. Shortstop will proceed as usual for a straight steal (take the throw and tag the runner out, then check the runner on third)
B. Bluff a throw to second base and try to catch runner on third leaning.
C. Throw hard toward second base and have pitcher cut off and throw to third base.
D. Throw hard toward second base and have the second baseman cut across in front of the base and attempt to catch the runner on third base breaking for the plate.

THE OUTFIELD

The outfield is the backbone of the defense. If the outfield fails, the team suffers. Unless they make a spectacular catch to save or end the game, the outfield is rarely applauded for their performances—this award is usually given to the pitchers—but without the outfielders doing their jobs, the outcome of the game would be quite different.

The outfielder should be thinking about his options on every pitch. When the ball comes to me, where are the runners and where do I make my throw?

If the ball is hit to another part of the field, where will the play develop? Who is responsible for backing up throws form the other area? Who do I back up?

One of the most common mistakes in the outfield is the failure to call a ball or to respect the fielder who has priority. This sometimes results in collisions that could take a player out of the game, possibly for the season. On fly balls that are the priority of someone else, those not involved should get into a backup position.

PRIORITY ON FLY BALLS (WHO CALLS WHO OFF AND WHEN)

On fly balls, in most cases, follow these basic rules:

1. Outfielders have priority over infielders.
2. Shortstop and second base have priority over first base, third base, and pitcher.
3. First base and third base have priority over the pitcher and catcher.
4. Catcher has priority over the pitcher.

PART IX

RULES OF THUMB AND TIPS FROM THE PAST

Categories of athlete's physical tools in order of importance by position:

Positions	1st	2nd	3rd	4th	5th
First Baseman Power	Hitting	Fielding	Arm	Speed	
Second Baseman	Fielding	Speed	Arm	Hitting	Power
Third Baseman	Hitting	Power	Fielding	Arm	Speed
Shortstop	Fielding	Arm	Speed	Hitting	Power
Catcher	Fielding	Arm	Hitting	Power	Speed
Pitcher	Velocity	Movement	Breaking	Control	
Left Fielder	Power	Hitting	Fielding	Arm	Speed
Center Fielder	Fielding	Hitting	Speed	Arm	Power
Right Fielder	Power	Arm	Fielding	Hitting	Speed

MAIN QUALITIES SOUGHT BY PROFESSIONAL SCOUTS IN YOUNG BALL PLAYERS

Professional Baseball Grading System.

1. Desire – Do they want to play?
2. Speed – Do they run well?
3. A Good Arm – Can they throw well?
4. Good Instincts and Reflexes – Do they react quickly?
5. A Quick Bat – Do they hit the ball sharply with a good swing?
6. Aggressive Attitude – Do they hustle at all times?
7. Aptitude – Do they learn quickly?
8. Physical Qualities – Height, weight, etc.
9. Character and Habits – Personality, personal problems, etc.

KEYS TO ATHLETIC SUCCESS

- Don't specialize in one sport too early.
- Cross training and participation in multiple sports is critical to full athletic development.
- Allow your body to recover and rest during the off-season.
- Proper nutrition and sleep.

STAGES OF OVERUSE INJURIES

- Pain in the affected area after physical activity.
- Pain during the activity without restricting performance.

- Pain during the activity that restricts performance.
- Chronic pain even at rest.

SIX RULES OF THUMB FOR PITCHERS

- Never give the first-ball hitter a good first pitch.
- The hitter who is worried about getting hit by a pitch is a prime candidate for a pitch that breaks away from him.
- A hitter who rocks back on his heels when taking a pitch may have trouble with outside pitch.
- The hitter who chases one pitch outside the strike zone is likely to chase a second.
- The lunge hitter (over strider) will have trouble with a curve or change-up because his weight is on the front foot.
- If a hitter guesses wrong and looks bad on a pitch, that pitch will stick in his mind the rest of the at bat; therefore, a pitcher's other pitches might become more effective.

TY COBB'S SIX KEYS TO SUCCESS

- Learn the fundamentals.
- Study and work at the game as if it were a science.
- Keep yourself in top physical shape.
- Make yourself as effective as possible.
- Get the desire to win.

  Developing an intense spirit to succeed.

BABE RUTH QUOTES

"Don't brag about winning, or cry about losing."

"The way a team plays as a whole determines their success. You may have the greatest bunch of individual stars in the world, but if they don't play together, the team won't be worth a dime."

MCCARTHY'S TEN COMMANDMENTS FOR SUCCESS IN BASEBALL*

**Joe McCarthy has the highest winning percentage as a major league manager.*

- Nobody ever becomes a ballplayer by walking after the ball.
- You will never become a .300 hitter unless you take the bat off your shoulder.
- If what you did yesterday still looks big to you, haven't done much today.
- Keep your head up and you may not have to keep it down.
- When you start to slide, SLIDE! He who changes his mind may have to change a good leg for a bad one.
- Do not alibi on bad hops. Anybody can field the good ones.
- Always run them out. You never can tell what might happen.
- Never quit!

- Do not find too much fault with the umpires. You cannot expect them to be as perfect as you are.
- A pitcher who has no control hasn't got anything.